# Pretty Hands
## & sweet feet

This library edition published in 2016 by Walter Foster Jr.,
an imprint of Quarto Publishing Group USA Inc.
6 Orchard Road, Suite 100
Lake Forest, CA 92630

Artwork and photographs on cover, back cover, and pages 6-11 and 16-37 © Sarah Waite.
Artwork and photographs on pages 12-15 and 38-59 © Samantha Tremlin. Artwork and
photographs on pages 60-93 © Katy Parsons. Artwork and photographs on pages 94-123 ©
Lindsey Williamson. Toenail artwork on pages 22, 30, 46, 54, 68, 76, 88, 102, 110, 122, and
photographs on page 128 © Penelope Yee. Special thanks to the following nail artists for
select inspiration gallery artwork: Jacki Gentry, Celine Peña, and Jessica Washick.
All other images © Shutterstock.
Copy Editor: Tracy Wilson-Burns
Page Layout: Kristin Krutsch

Distributed in the United States and Canada by
Lerner Publisher Services
241 First Avenue North
Minneapolis, MN 55401 U.S.A.
www.lernerbooks.com

First Library Edition

Library of Congress Cataloging-in-Publication Data

Names: Quarto Publishing Limited, publisher, author.
Title: Pretty hands & sweet feet : paint your way through a coloful variety
   of crazy-cute nail art designs, step by step.
Other titles: Pretty hands and sweet feet | Paint your way through a coloful
   variety of crazy-cute nail art designs, step by step
Description: Lake Forest [California] : Quarto Publishing Group, USA, Inc., [2015]
Identifiers: LCCN 2015051214 | ISBN 9781942875123 (hardcover)
Subjects:  LCSH: Nail art (Manicuring)--Juvenile literature.
Classification: LCC TT958.3 .P74 2015 | DDC 646.7/27--dc23
LC record available at http://lccn.loc.gov/2015051214

Printed in USA
9 8 7 6 5 4 3 2 1

# Pretty Hands
## & sweet feet

Paint your way through a colorful variety of
crazy-cute nail art designs—step by step

Sarah Waite, Samantha Tremlin,
Katy Parsons, and Lindsey Williamson
with toenail designs by Penelope Yee

# TABLE OF CONTENTS

# TOOLS OF THE TRADE

The tools and materials on the following pages will help you get started creating the stylish nail art in this book. You can find most of these materials online or at your local beauty supply store or pharmacy.

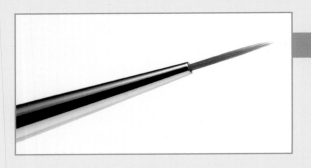

## Striping Brush

A nail art striping brush has long, thin bristles, ideal for creating smooth, skinny lines.

## Detailing Brush

A detailing brush has shorter bristles for precise, controlled strokes.

## Fan Brush

The bristles on a fan brush are spread out in the shape of a fan. They are often used for a brushy, loose effect and can be used for a quick gradient design.

## Cleanup Brush

Cleanup brushes are great for making sure the edges of your manicure are smooth and clean. Dip the brush in acetone, and swipe it around your cuticle or along the nail walls for a flawless finish.

## Dotting Tool

Dotting tools have a metal ball on the end. They are dipped into nail polish and then used to create perfect dots on the nail. Dotting tools come in various sizes to best suit your needs.

## Tape

Tape is often used as a stencil in nail art. There are different benefits to each type of tape. Experiment with washi, Scotch® tape, and painter's tape to find your favorite.

## Striping Tape

Striping tape is a very thin nail art tape that often comes in multicolored metallic finishes. It can be used as a stencil or left on the nail as a decoration.

## Toothpicks

Toothpicks are a great nail art tool for detail work and can stand in as both a detail brush or a dotting tool if needed.

## Makeup Sponge

This wedge-shaped cosmetic sponge is a nail artist favorite for creating smooth, blended bases and flawless gradients.

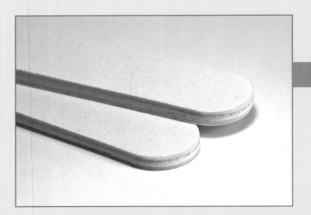

## Nail File

Files are used to shape your nails. The higher the number, the finer the grit. For natural nails, choose a 180 grit or higher.

## Cotton Swabs

Cotton swabs can be useful for cleaning up any polish that may have gotten on your skin during the nail art process. If you're feeling creative, try them as a dotting tool or brush substitute as well!

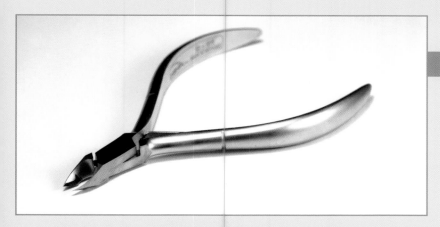

## Cuticle Nippers

Cuticle nippers are a tool used to trim dead tissue away from the nail area. Use with caution: most nails don't require nippers at all.

## Clippers

Clippers are used to shorten the nail. For best results, clip the nail first, and then use a file to seal and smooth the edge.

## Cuticle Pusher

A cuticle pusher is a metal implement that can be used to push back the cuticle and remove dead tissue from the nail plate. Combine it with a cuticle-softening product for best results.

## Rhinestones

These imitation gems come in many colors and are used to decorate the nail.

## Studs

These nail art decorations are made from metal. They are sometimes decorated with patterns or prints.

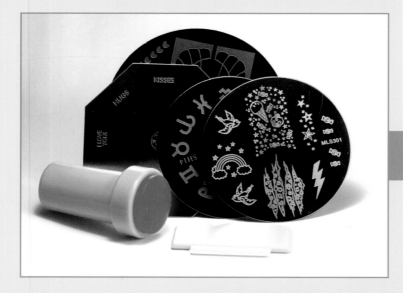

## Stamper & Stamping Plates

Nail art stamping is an alternative to freehand nail art that uses etched metal plates and a rubber stamper to transfer designs to the nail.

## Polishes

There are many different finishes of nail polish!

- **CRÈME** Solid colors without any shimmer or other particles.
- **SHIMMER** Similar to a crème polish, but with a sparkly shimmer.
- **JELLY** A translucent polish with a slight tint of color.
- **GLITTER** Sparkly polish that may be in either a tinted or clear base.
- **METALLIC** Polishes with a smooth, reflective finish.

## Base & Topcoat

Base coat and topcoat are important for every manicure! Base coat is used to protect the nail and keep the polish from chipping, while topcoat seals and smooths your finished nail art design.

## Acetone

This colorless solvent is used in many nail polish removers.

# TECHNIQUES & TIPS

Get comfortable with these basic techniques,
and you'll become a nail art pro in no time!

## Fine Lines

To create fine lines and striped
designs, use a striping brush at
least 8 mm long and as thin as
possible. For straight lines, the
longer and thinner the better!

## QUICK TIPS

- For the best results, keep the nail polish you're working with at a thin consistency. Use a piece of scrap paper or palette to hold the nail polish, and add a drop of acetone or nail polish remover when things start to thicken up.

- Use a very light hand. You can always build up more color later, but it's hard to remove polish once applied.

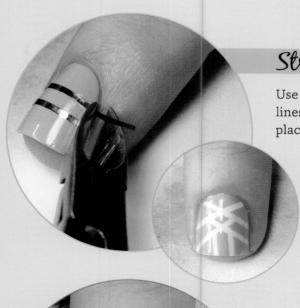

## Striping Tape

Use striping tape as a decoration or to create stenciled lines and designs. A pair of tweezers will really help to place the tape exactly where you need it.

### QUICK TIPS

- For the crispest lines possible, remove the tape while the polish is still wet.
- When using striping tape on top of your design as an accent, seal with lots of topcoat (especially at the edges) to prevent it from peeling off.

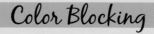

## Color Blocking

Use washi or Scotch tape to create a layered design. Experiment with shapes, angles, and color combinations to create a truly unique look.

### QUICK TIPS

- Allow your base coat to dry completely before applying the tape. A fast-drying topcoat will help speed up the process.
- Smooth down the edges of the tape completely; otherwise, polish will creep underneath and leave a wobbly line.
- Stick the tape to the back of your hand to remove some of the stickiness before using it on your nail. This makes it easier to peel away and reduces the chances of removing the polish underneath.

## Rhinestones & Studs

Rhinestones and studs add a bit of flare to your otherwise plain manicure. Jazz up your nail art designs with these gems as a finishing touch.

**QUICK TIPS**

- Use a very small dot of nail glue to affix the stud to your nail.
- Use a thick layer of topcoat to seal it on.
- You can buy wax pencils, which will help pick up and place your studs. A felt-tip pen will do the job too.

## Gradient

Create a smooth transition between colors using a makeup sponge. Use a toothpick to swirl the colors together on a piece of scrap paper first to "pre-blend" your gradient.

**QUICK TIPS**

- It's best to build up your gradient in thin layers. Leave plenty of drying time between each layer to make sure you don't smudge the color.
- It's harder to blend thick nail polish into a gradient. If you can't get the blend right, try using a thinner polish.

## Stamping

Try using a stamping kit to transfer intricate designs to your nails from etched metal plates. Drop stamping polish onto the plates, scrape away the excess, and use the rubber stamper to transfer the art.

### QUICK TIPS

- The key to the perfect stamp is moving quickly. Practice makes perfect, and once you know all the steps, you'll whiz through!

- An old credit card is often the best tool to use for scraping away excess polish from the stamping plate.

- Get creative by using more than one shade of nail polish when you stamp. Blend them together before scraping, or split them straight down the middle for some interesting effects.

- Most polishes will stamp over a light color, but when it comes to stamping over a dark shade, it gets a bit tricky to find the right stamping polish. Most chrome-finish nail polishes will work, and you can even buy nail polishes that are specially formulated for stamping.

## Cleanup

When finished with any design, use a cleanup brush dipped in pure acetone to clean up your cuticles and around the edges of your nail bed. Find a brush that works best for you. Some people prefer an angled brush, while others like to use a slim, pointed brush. Pure acetone works best for cleaning up around your nails and can be purchased at your local pharmacy. Always use a moisturizing cuticle cream after cleanup to keep your nails in good condition.

# Sarah Waite

## CHALKBOARD NAILS

### WWW.CHALKBOARDNAILS.COM

My name is Sarah, and I'm the nail artist behind *Chalkboard Nails*, a nail art–focused blog that features wild to refined freehand designs, simple to advanced nail art pictorials and video tutorials, and up-to-date nail polish swatches and reviews. I've been fortunate to have my work featured on the *TODAY* show, *Nail'd It!* on Oxygen, OPI's Virtual Nail Studio, *Redbook Magazine*, and more.

I've always been interested in the creative arts. I earned my BFA in photography, where I was exposed to a wide range of artistic mediums, including drawing, painting, metalworking, and printmaking. However, my journey into nail art didn't begin until a few years ago when I saw a leopard print tutorial and just had to try it. I've been absolutely crazy about nail art ever since!

I love nail art because the canvases are so small, yet the possibilities are endless. My photography background has definitely influenced the development of my unique style. My designs are frequently inspired by color, patterns, textures, and elements of pop culture. I always keep a sketchbook nearby to jot down my ideas before they get away from me.

Spurred on by the urging of my friends and peers, I quit my job to become a licensed nail technician. It's pretty incredible to consider that what started out as a hobby has grown into such a huge part of my life. I've gone from an enthusiast to a pro, and I can't wait to see where nail art takes me next!

# Picnic Chic

## The breeze in your hair...

The grass under your feet...Who doesn't love a picnic on a beautiful day? Now you can channel those vibes with this chic gingham nail art tutorial. Don't worry, the little ant just wants to say hello!

## What You'll Need:

**Brushes—**
- Striping brush
- Detailing brush
- Dotting tool

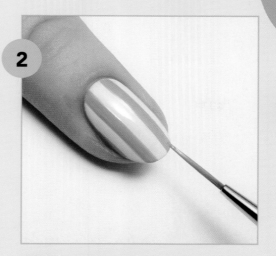

**STEP 1** Prep your nails with a base coat, and then paint your nails with two to three coats of white crème nail polish.

**STEP 2** Using a peachy nail polish and a nail art striping brush, paint two thick stripes down the middle of your nails. If you have room, continue the stripes to the edges of your nails.

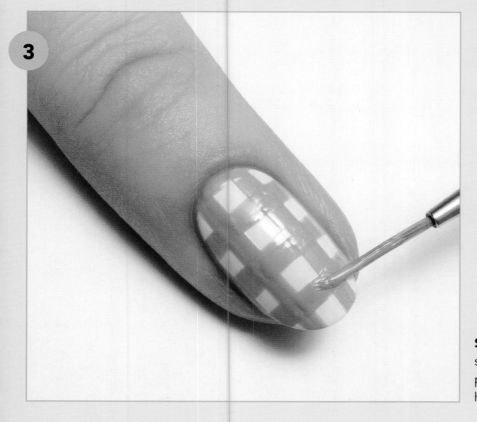

**STEP 3** Using the same peach polish, paint evenly spaced horizontal stripes.

**STEP 5** Finish with a topcoat for seal and shine.

**STEP 4** Use a nail art detailing brush with red nail polish to paint small squares at the intersections of your horizontal and vertical stripes.

## Ant Accent Nail

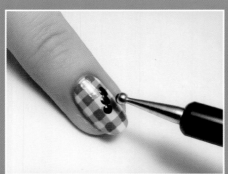

### Quick Tip

When applying a topcoat, use a light touch to avoid smearing your nail art. You may want to put a bead of topcoat on the end of a brush and lightly float it over your nails.

**STEP 1** Using a nail art dotting tool and black nail polish, place three large black dots in a line.

**STEP 2** Grab your detailing brush, and add three small lines coming off each side of the middle dot and two short antennae off the top dot. Finish with a topcoat for seal and shine.

# Music Lover

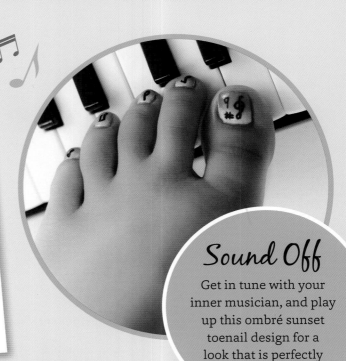

## Express yourself

with these colorful, musical nails! Whether you're a country gal or a pop princess, these cute music notes will have you humming a cheerful tune.

### What You'll Need:

**Brushes—**
- Large dotting tool
- Detailing brush

## Sound Off

Get in tune with your inner musician, and play up this ombré sunset toenail design for a look that is perfectly on key.

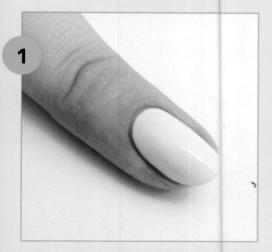

**STEP 1** Apply a base coat, and then paint your nails with two to three coats of a white créme nail polish.

**STEP 2** Cut a small strip of a wedge-shaped cosmetic sponge. Paint three stripes of polish directly onto the sponge, each about one-third the length of your nail. Make sure there is ample polish on the sponge. I used aqua, purple, and hot pink.

**STEP 3** Lightly and quickly tap the sponge up and down your nail. Try to use the taps to blur the areas between the colors. Repeat on all of your nails, refilling the stripes of polish on the sponge after every couple of nails. Repeat two or three times until you are happy with the brightness of your gradient.

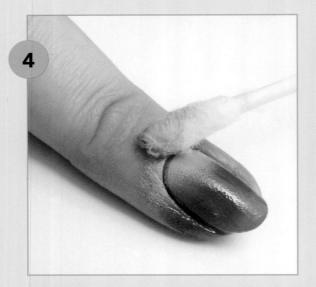

**STEP 4** Take a cotton swab, and dip it in nail polish remover. Use the swab to clean up any polish on your fingers.

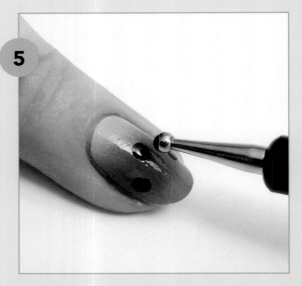

**STEP 5** Use a dotting tool to place large dots of black nail polish wherever you want your music notes.

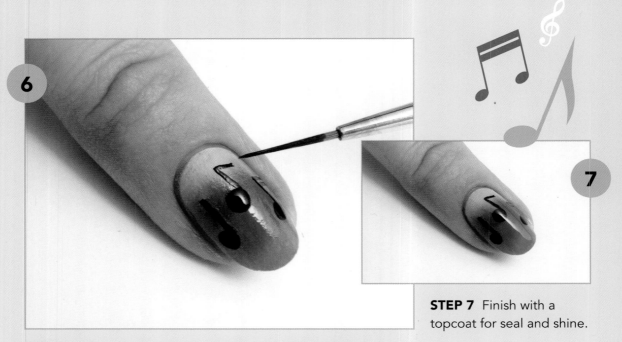

**STEP 6** Use a detailing brush to add the music note stems. Feel free to vary the types of notes!

**STEP 7** Finish with a topcoat for seal and shine.

# Wood Grain

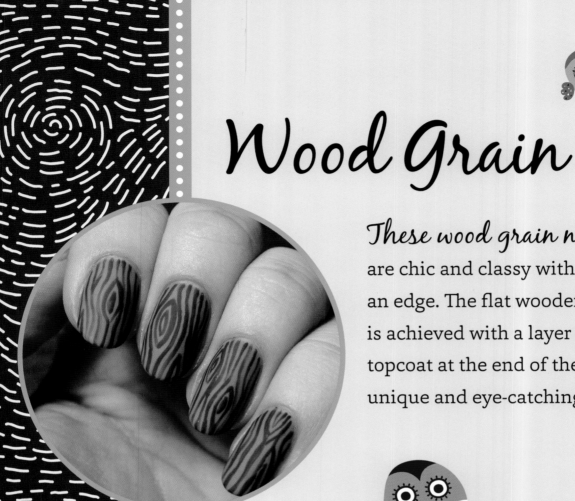

These wood grain nails are chic and classy with a bit of an edge. The flat wooden finish is achieved with a layer of matte topcoat at the end of the design for a unique and eye-catching manicure.

## What You'll Need:

Brushes—
• Small detailing brush

**STEP 1** Apply a base coat, and then paint your nails with two to three coats of caramel-colored nail polish.

**STEP 2** Using a slightly darker brown shade and a small detailing brush, paint an eye-shaped marking near the center of your nail.

**STEP 3** Add a smaller eye shape inside the larger one.

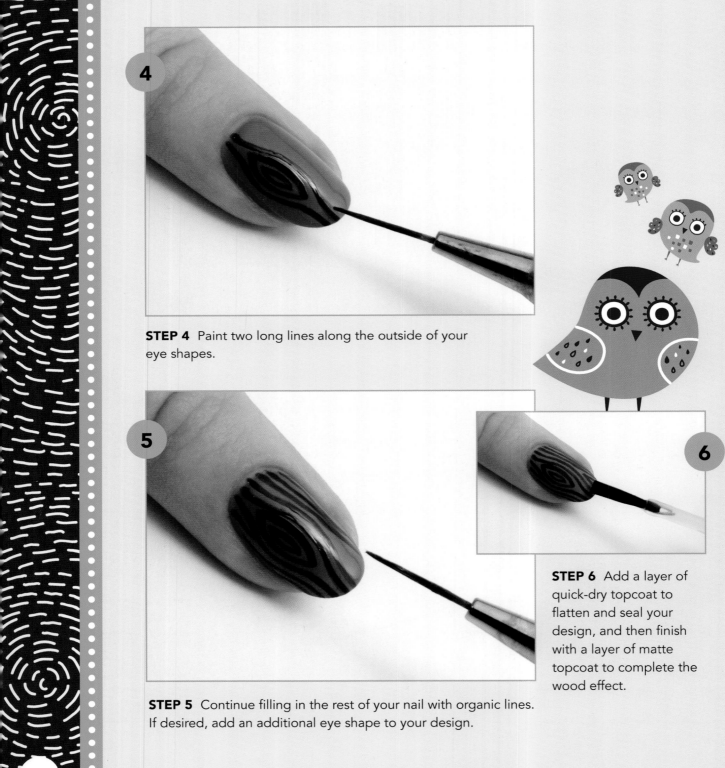

**STEP 4** Paint two long lines along the outside of your eye shapes.

**STEP 5** Continue filling in the rest of your nail with organic lines. If desired, add an additional eye shape to your design.

**STEP 6** Add a layer of quick-dry topcoat to flatten and seal your design, and then finish with a layer of matte topcoat to complete the wood effect.

# Tie-dye

## Embrace the summer

with this free-spirited tie-dye design! Nothing says fun quite like neon rainbow spirals on your tips.

### Groovy, Baby

Give peace a chance! These psychedelic toenails are perfect for a summer rock concert or for just hanging out on the beach.

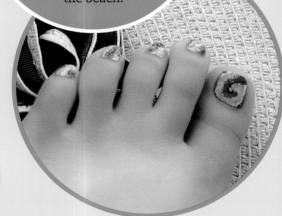

## What You'll Need:

### Brushes—
• Detailing brush

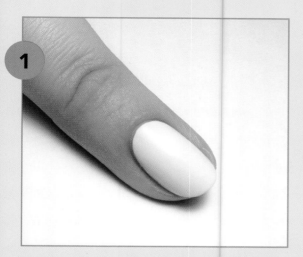

**STEP 1** Apply a base coat, and then paint your nails with two to three coats of white nail polish.

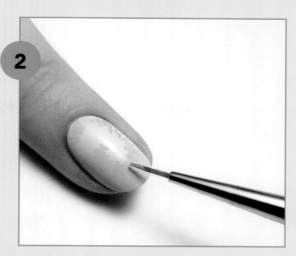

**STEP 2** Using a small detailing brush or toothpick and neon yellow polish, create small dashes spiraling outward from the center of your nail. The dashes should be irregular in size for a more natural, dyed look.

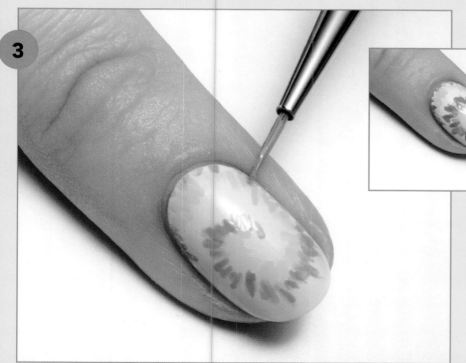

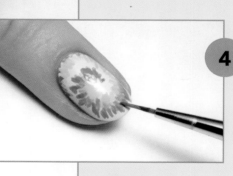

**STEP 4** Continue to build your spiral by adding a layer of bright blue on the outside of the green.

**STEP 3** Grab a neon green polish and continue adding dashes along the outside of the yellow spiral. They should overlap the yellow slightly.

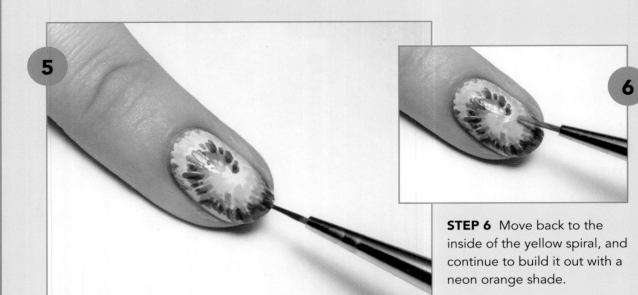

**STEP 5** Add a spiral of neon magenta around the outside of the blue.

**STEP 6** Move back to the inside of the yellow spiral, and continue to build it out with a neon orange shade.

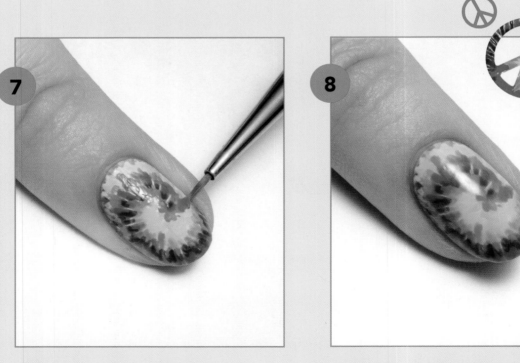

**STEP 7** Finish the spiral with a layer of neon red inside of the orange.

**STEP 8** Complete the look by smoothing everything out with a layer of topcoat.

# Watercolor Dots

## Feeling whimsical?

Try this simple polka-dot nail art! The color palette includes shades of cream, mint, and gold for a vintage feel.

## What You'll Need:

**Brushes—**
- Wide nail art brush
- Medium dotting tool

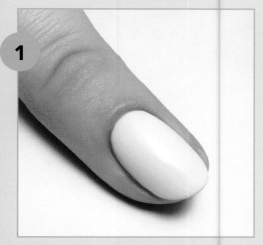

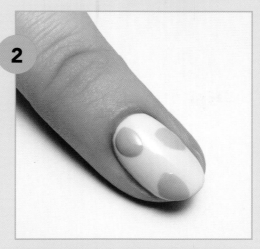

**STEP 1** Apply a base coat, and then paint your nails with two to three coats of an ivory nail polish. Seal it in with a topcoat to protect it from the next steps.

**STEP 2** Using the brush from the nail polish, dab on three spots of a sky blue shade.

**STEP 3** Repeat step 2 with a mint green shade.

**STEP 4** Grab a wide nail art brush and saturate it with 100 percent pure acetone. Lightly dab the brush with acetone over your green and blue spots while they are still wet, creating a wash of color.

**STEP 5** Using a dotting tool and gold polish, begin by adding a row of dots down the center of your nail.

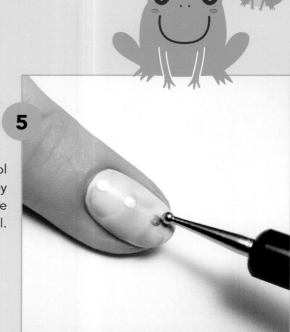

**STEP 6** Continue adding gold dots until your entire nail is filled. Stagger the rows so the dots alternate. Finish the look with a topcoat for seal and shine.

# Samantha Tremlin

## THE NAILASAURUS

### WWW.THENAILASAURUS.COM

I'm Samantha, but everyone calls me Sammy! I live in a picturesque area called South Wales in the United Kingdom. By day I work in social media and marketing, but by night (and on the weekends) you'll find me hard at work on my nail art blog, *The Nailasaurus.*

I've always been crafty and creative, but I never really found my passion until I stumbled across nail blogs and started experimenting with my own nail art. Once I started to explore the subject a bit more online, I was dazed by the endless possibilities. There's always more to learn in the world of nail art, and most nail art techniques can be mastered in a very short period of time if you put in the practice.

Nail art quickly became an obsession! I launched *The Nailasaurus* just a few months after investing in my own little nail art kit that consisted of a few stamping plates and a little set of brushes. It served as the perfect creative outlet to combine all of my hobbies—nail art, photography, and the Internet—into one. My original idea was to keep a kind of "nail art journal" by simply posting my daily creations, but as my knowledge and skill set grew, so did my blog. I started creating tutorials, product reviews, and even the occasional video!

My personal nail art style is very minimalist, and I like playing with striking color combinations to really make an impression. I look for inspiration in the world around me in everything from fashion to nature. Nail art really is artwork for the individual, and that's why I love it so much.

# Dotty Florals

Bust out the flower power with this quick-and-easy floral look that's perfect for when you're in a rush but still want to rock fabulous nails.

## What You'll Need:

**Brushes—**
- Medium dotting tool

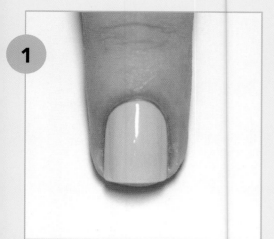

**STEP 1** Paint on a light base color to get started, and wait until it's dry to the touch.

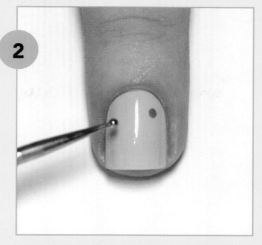

**STEP 2** With a slightly darker shade, use a dotting tool to start your flower with a single dot.

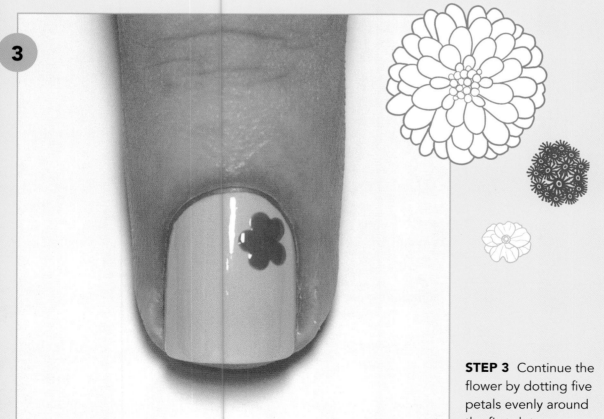

**STEP 3** Continue the flower by dotting five petals evenly around the first dot.

**4**

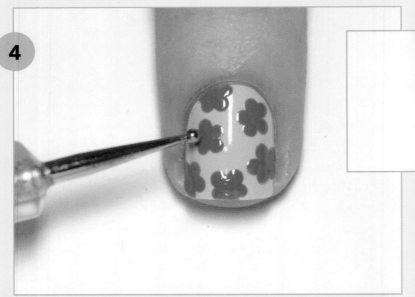

**5**

**STEP 5** Use a contrasting color to add a single dot to the center of each flower.

**STEP 4** Repeat all over your nail until you're happy with the look.

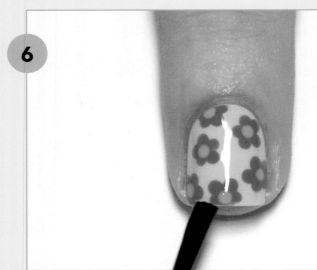

**6**

## Quick Tip

Try a different color scheme, or use flowers of assorted colors! You can also try using a larger dotting tool to create one or two accent flowers on your thumb or ring finger.

**STEP 6** Add a clear topcoat for a glossy finish and longer-lasting mani.

# Dragon Fruit

For this design, I was inspired by a polka-dot dragon fruit that's been sliced straight down the middle. This little fruit looks just as sweet on your nails as the real thing tastes!

## What You'll Need:

### Brushes—
- Dotting tool
- Small detailing brush

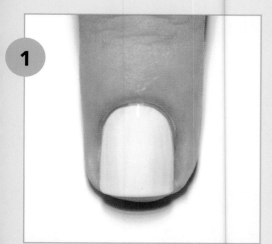

**STEP 1** Start with a white polish as your base color. Use as many smooth coats as you need to get a bright white finish. Wait for 10 minutes or so until the polish is completely dry to the touch.

## Quick Tip

If you don't have a dotting tool handy, there are plenty of household items that will make a good alternative. The end of a bobby pin, a matchstick, or even the tip of ballpoint pen will do the job when you're in a pinch!

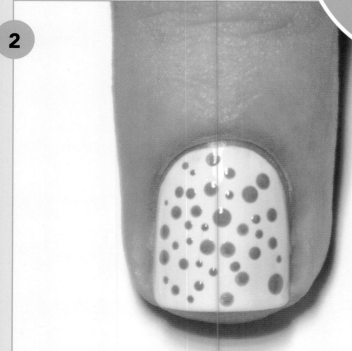

**STEP 2** Using a dotting tool, add lots of randomly sized light gray dots over the white base. You can also scatter some black dots in there too for extra contrast.

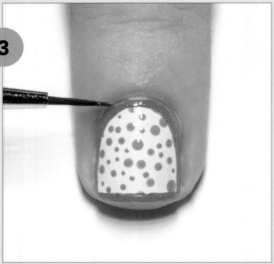

**3**

**4**

**STEP 3** Take a small nail art brush, and draw a frame around the edge of your nail using bright pink nail polish.

**STEP 4** To finish up, just add a layer or two of your favorite topcoat to give it a glossy shine and make it last.

## Jungle Love

If your fingers can get wild and crazy, so can your toes! Stretch this polka dot fruit design from the tips of your toes to the roots of your nail beds.

# Tricolor Tribal

## This freehanded tribal

nail art calls for three shades of
polish and one striping brush. Try
it with complementing colors for
an easy-breezy look, or go with
contrasting shades for the full
wow factor.

### What You'll Need:

### Brushes—
- Striping brush
- Dotting tool

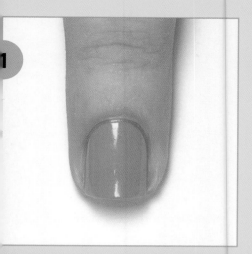

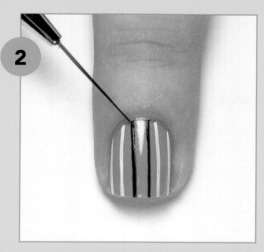

**STEP 1** Lay down a bright base color, and wait 10 to 15 minutes for it to dry.

**STEP 2** Using a striping brush and two different colors, paint six equally spaced stripes starting at your cuticles and working toward the tips.

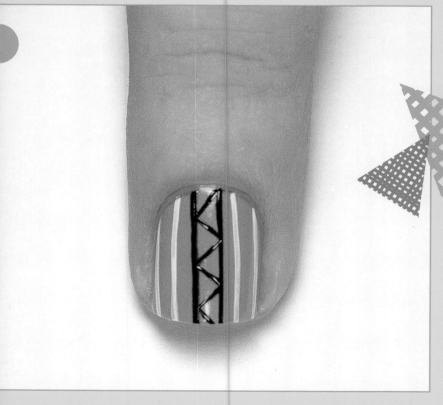

**STEP 3** Go back with the striping brush and paint some zigzags between the two center lines.

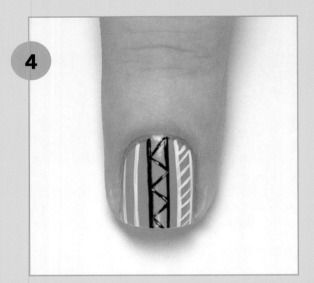

**STEP 4** Next add a dashed pattern between two of the lines on the right side.

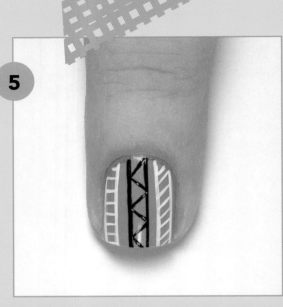

**STEP 5** Finally create some squares between the two lines on the left side.

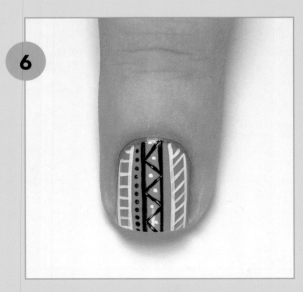

**STEP 6** As a finishing touch, use a dotting tool to add some polka dots.

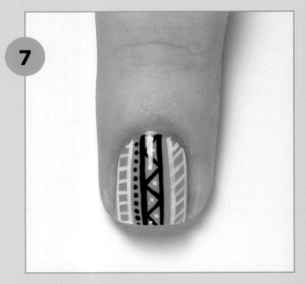

**STEP 7** Add your favorite topcoat for a smooth, glossy finish—and you're good to go!

## Quick Tip

Mix up your color combinations for some stunning results!

# Strawberry Stripes

These nails are ideal for a picnic at the park and give off a real summer vibe. Try adding a few more fruity favorites for a mix-and-match mani.

## What You'll Need:

### Brushes—
- Striping brush
- Detailing brush

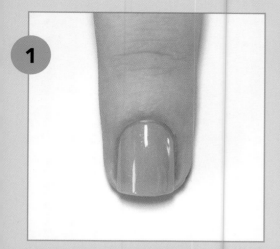

**STEP 1** Paint on a pink base color and let it dry.

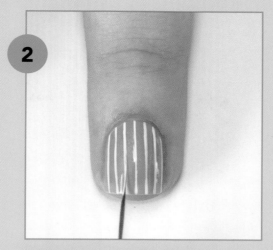

**STEP 2** Using the longest, thinnest striping brush you can find, add some pinstripes using white nail polish.

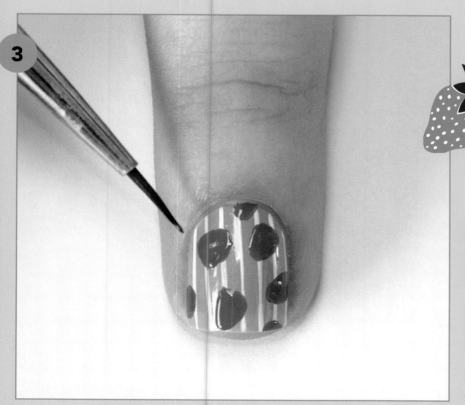

**STEP 3** Use a detailing brush to paint some strawberry outlines with red polish. Aim for slightly rounded triangles—or slightly squashed circles depending how you want to look at it!

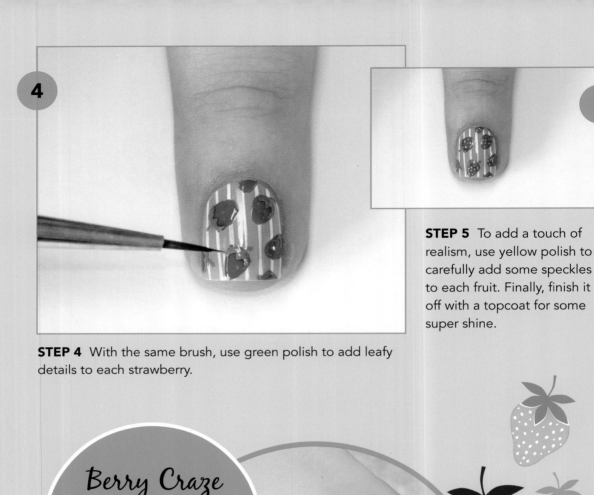

**STEP 4** With the same brush, use green polish to add leafy details to each strawberry.

**STEP 5** To add a touch of realism, use yellow polish to carefully add some speckles to each fruit. Finally, finish it off with a topcoat for some super shine.

### Berry Craze

Help yourself to more strawberries with this berry-inspired toenail design. Your piggies never looked so sweet!

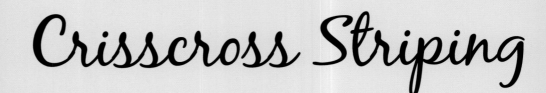

# Crisscross Striping

**Grab the striping tape** for this look inspired by the timeless art deco styles from the roaring 1920s. With just a bit of glitter peeking through, this nail art adds the perfect amount of glitz and glam to any outfit.

## What You'll Need:

**Brushes—**
- Striping tape
- Tweezers

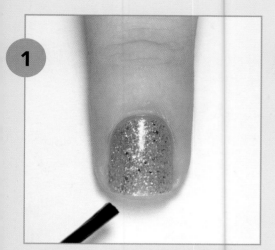

**STEP 1** Layer up your sparkliest glitter polish, and add a thin coat of a quick-dry topcoat to make sure it's completely dry before moving on to the next step.

**STEP 2** Using a pair of tweezers, place some striping tape in a large X over the center of your nail. Add a V shape near the cuticle as an accent.

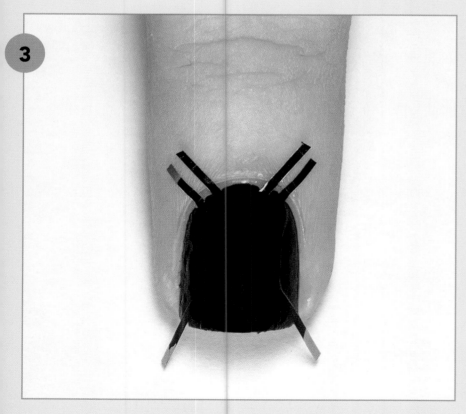

**STEP 3** Using black nail polish, paint over the striping tape.

**STEP 4** Before the black polish has a chance to dry, use the tweezers to peel away the striping tape.

**STEP 5** Wait a little while, and then go over the design with your favorite topcoat. For a perfect finish, you may want to go back for a second helping of topcoat to fill in the ridges where you peeled back the striping tape.

## Striping Tape Do's and Don'ts

- Tweezers are striping tape's best friend! They're really helpful for applying and removing the tape.

- Only use striping tape on nail polish that's completely dry.

- For the crispest lines, peel away the striping tape while the polish on top is still wet. If the polish dries before you remove the tape, you'll end up leaving rough edges. It helps to work on just one nail at a time.

- Use plenty of topcoat to ensure a super-smooth finish.

# Katy Parsons
## NAILED IT

WWW.BLOGNAILEDIT.CO

I'm Katy, and I created my nail art blog, *Nailed It*, on my bed beside a sweet little kitten named Nugget. I started my foray into nail art in 2010, and if you read *Nailed It* now, you'll see mostly freehand nail art designs.

After I graduated college, I moved to San Francisco where, housebound by winter weather, I tried stamping plates for the first time and became hooked. After scouring the Internet for more styles, I saw that girls were sharing their nail art on their blogs, and people were excited to read them! So I came up with a catchy name, posted my first design, and from there it exploded. Now I am a nail technician for a spa full of clients who are beginning to love nail art as much as you and I! It's a dream come true, but it's not something I'd ever dreamed of doing.

I was inspired by other girls to try something that wasn't anything like what I went to school for. I majored in environmental studies and minored with a design emphasis in theater (art has always been a big part of my life). I now live in Boulder, Colorado, which offers some of the prettiest sights to be seen. My creative space is either outside on my deck beneath a 50-year-old tree or inside at my desk listening to music and doodling. I like to combine things from different worlds in my designs, such as leaves stuck to cars, and I use my library of over 1,000 nail polishes to create patterns from those color and texture combinations. Patterns and details are my favorite designs, but nail art inspiration can come from anywhere, anytime. So get creative, get fun, and get painting—you have 20 tiny canvases to paint!

# Dainty Dandelion

**Folklore says that picking** a dandelion and blowing its seeds into the wind has the power to grant you a wish! If you've ever wished that you could be an excellent nail artist, you can thank your dandelion friends and start practicing this easy, out-of-the-box floral design. You'll "blow" your friends away when they see your skills.

## What You'll Need:

### Brushes—
- Detailing brush
- Dotting tool

**STEP 1** Apply a base coat and two coats of light blue nail polish.

**STEP 2** Place a couple of drops of black nail polish on a piece of scrap paper. Dip your detailing brush in the polish, and then paint a line from your cuticle to the center of your nail.

**STEP 3** Paint two smaller lines coming off the tip of the line as shown.

**STEP 4** Fill in around the smaller lines, creating a fan of small lines as shown.

**STEP 5** With a dotting tool, add little circles to the ends of your small lines.

**STEP 6** With the detailing brush, add little lines randomly around your flower. This makes your seeds look like they're blowing in the breeze.

**STEP 7** Finish your artwork by placing circles on the ends of your blowing seeds, and seal the design with topcoat to make it last!

# Beautiful Bows

### Using a detailing brush

is an easy way to draw cute, detailed icons on your nails, including these adorable pink bows—perfect for springtime. Not confident in your freehand painting skills? Try using a black felt-tip pen to outline the bow instead. The details will have your friends asking if you used stickers!

## What You'll Need:

### Brushes—
- Large dotting tool
- Detailing brush

**STEP 1** Apply a base coat and two coats of light green nail polish.

**STEP 2** Place a couple of drops of pink nail polish on a piece of scrap paper. Dip your dotting tool in the polish, and then place a dot in the center of your nail.

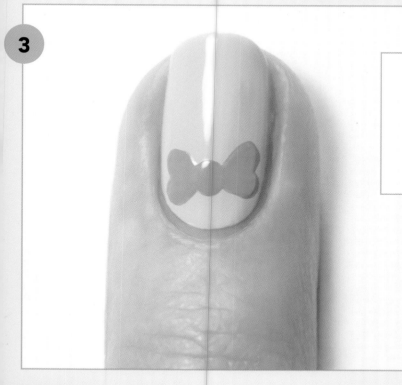

**STEP 3** Use a detailing brush to paint pink heart shapes coming from the middle of the dot.

**STEP 4** Place a few drops of black nail polish on a piece of scrap paper, and outline the shapes as shown with the detailing brush. You can also use a fine black felt-tip pen if that's easier for you!

**5**

**6**

**STEP 5** Paint elongated ovals near the base of the bow. This gives dimension to the bow and makes it look like a sticker!

**STEP 6** Paint little lines coming from the center knot of the bow for even more dimension, and finish your design with topcoat.

## Wrap It Up

Give yourself the gift of crazy-cute toenails, and wrap those toes in sparkling ribbons and bows. Try red and green polish for a festive holiday look!

# Retro Scales

Geometric patterns are a fantastic way to practice your line skills, and this one lends itself to improvement because you can simply cover up your mistakes if you make any. Plus, changing the colors of each scale can completely update and change the look and feel of the design!

## What You'll Need:

### Brushes—
• Detailing brush

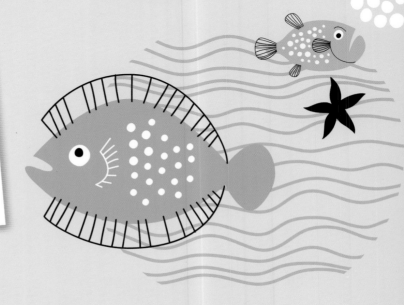

**1**

**STEP 1** Apply a base coat and two coats of white nail polish.

**2**

**STEP 2** Place a couple drops of black nail polish on a piece of scrap paper, and then dip your detailing brush in it. Paint a straight line right down the middle of your nail.

**3**

**STEP 3** Starting at the base of the straight line near your cuticle, paint curved lines moving out toward the sides.

**STEP 4** Paint several other lines in the same direction all the way up the middle line as shown.

**STEP 5** Place drops of all the other colors on the piece of scrap paper. Fill in some of the scales with alternating colors. There's no rhyme or reason to how you choose which colors go in which scales, just do what looks nice to you!

**STEP 6** With your detailing brush, go over your black lines again to cover colors that bled onto the outlines. This makes the design really bold! Finish up the design with a topcoat and enjoy!

# Covered in Camo

### Attention!

I don't know, but I've been told

Camo nails are mighty bold!

I don't know, but it's been said

Painting these will knock 'em dead!

Sound off—Color Club®!

Sound off—OPI®!

Grab your tools and let's apply!

## What You'll Need:

**Brushes—**
• Medium dotting tool

**STEP 1** Apply a base coat, and then use two coats of army green nail polish.

## Quick Tip

Be sure to let each layer of nail polish dry before adding the next. This will keep the colors and shapes bright and defined.

**STEP 2** Place a couple of drops of mint green on a piece of scrap paper. Dip your dotting tool in the mint green, and place a dot on your nail, lightly dragging it so it creates an uneven, messy shape. Repeat this a few times around the nail, dragging in different directions.

**3**

**STEP 3** Now repeat step 2 with your next lightest color. Overlap the colors on top of each other.

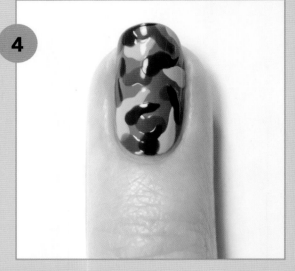

**4**

**STEP 4** Repeat again with your darkest color. Fill in some of the areas that expose the base color, but leave some open so you can see all four colors. To complete your cool camo mani and make it last, finish with a topcoat!

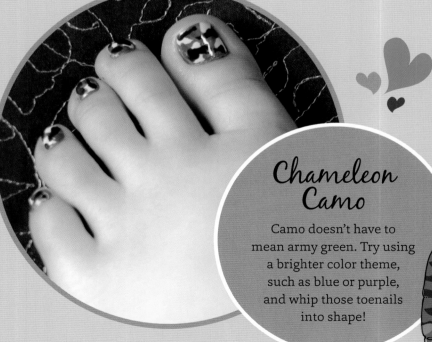

## Chameleon Camo

Camo doesn't have to mean army green. Try using a brighter color theme, such as blue or purple, and whip those toenails into shape!

# Charming Cherry Blossoms

**Picture yourself lying under** a cherry tree, basking in the sun, and gazing up at the bright blue sky. As the flower petals float down across your forehead, you wake up and realize you're not under a beautiful tree—but the flower petals are on your nails! And they're just as beautiful!

## What You'll Need:

**Brushes—**
- Small dotting tool
- Medium dotting tool
- Detailing brush

**STEP 1** After applying your base coat, add two coats of light blue polish to each nail.

**STEP 2** Drop a small dot of brown polish on a piece of scrap paper. With a detailing brush, paint lines that are wavy and jagged to look like branches. Start at the edge of your nail and paint toward the other side.

**STEP 3** With your medium dotting tool and light pink polish, create little flower shapes on the branches. They don't have to be perfect or even.

**STEP 4** In the middle of each flower, use a clean detailing brush to paint little lines in a circle with a dark pink polish.

**STEP 5** Grab a small dotting tool or a toothpick. Place a few dots of purple polish in the center of each flower.

**STEP 6** Clean your detailing brush again, and paint little leaf shapes with green polish. Place the brush lightly near the branch, and then quickly swipe away, creating small teardrop shapes. Preserve your work with a quick-dry topcoat.

# Mod Petals

**Make mama proud with** this retro nod to mod. This will take her back to the miniskirts and platforms of her former years, but you won't be dated with your design. Retro is in—and you will be too!

## What You'll Need:

### Brushes—
- Small dotting tool
- Detailing brush

**STEP 1** After applying your base coat, add two coats of white polish to each nail.

**STEP 2** Drop a small dot of yellow polish on a piece of scrap paper. Use your detailing brush to paint a small dot about two-thirds of the way up your nail. Around that dot, add little curved lines. Work your way around the circle, trying not to connect any of the lines. Keep going until you have a nice size flower.

**STEP 3** Clean your brush, and pick up a little bit of light green. Paint little leaf shapes coming off of the flower. It's up to you how many you make, but leave some open space for step 5.

**STEP 4** Clean your brush again, and dip it in dark green. Quickly swipe your detailing brush around the outside of the leaves to give them some depth. Quick, fast strokes create an effortless look.

**STEP 5** In the open space you left in step 3, paint another quick, long line coming off of the flower in dark green.

**STEP 6** With a thin detailing brush and a steady hand, add little lines coming off of that long line.

**STEP 7** Dip a small dotting tool in dark green, and place dots on the end of the little lines and scattered around the center of your flower. With these last details, the flower should come to life! Don't forget to finish with a quick-dry topcoat to seal the design!

# Perfect Puppy Paws

**As popular as animal print** has become for nail art, there aren't enough Fido finger designs. Dogs may be "man's best friend," but perfect puppy paws are better suited for *princesses!*

## What You'll Need:

### Brushes—
- Medium dotting tool
- Large dotting tool

**STEP 1** Apply your base coat and two coats of fuchsia.

**STEP 2** Drop a little white onto a scrap piece of paper, and pick some of it up with the large dotting tool. Place two big dots side by side at the base of your nail.

**STEP 4** Connect the first two dots by filling in the empty space between them, creating a nice, smooth line. Using your polish's brush may help with this step if you're having trouble with the dotting tool.

**STEP 3** Place another large dot above the first two, right between them.

**5**

**6**

**STEP 5** Use the medium dotting tool to add four little toes above the pad of the paw print.

**STEP 6** If you have more room on your nail, repeat steps 2 through 5 with black. On some nails I used both colors, and on other nails I just used one color. It's fun to mix it up across your nails.

## Puppy Love

Need a pawtastic pedicure? Look no further. Try these puppy prints in any color, and your friends won't stop howling about them!

## Quick Tip

Polish off your paws
with a clear topcoat for
a longer-lasting look.

# Silly Skulls

Take the trick out of "trick or treat" with these easy, not-so-scary skulls. This is a design for the hard-punk-rockin' chick in all of us!

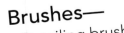

## What You'll Need:

**Brushes—**
• Detailing brush

**STEP 1** Apply your base coat and two coats of white polish.

**STEP 2** Drop some black polish on scrap paper, and then paint two little diagonal lines with a detailing brush near the free edge of your nail. You will fill these in later, so don't worry about perfection.

**STEP 3** Paint a horizontal line connecting the two diagonal lines.

**4**

**STEP 4** Now carefully fill in all the space between the lines you made and the free edge of your nail. The leftover white area creates the shape of your skull.

**5**

**STEP 5** Give your skull a nose by painting a small, upside-down heart in the middle. Give yourself enough room for teeth below and eyes above.

**6**

**STEP 6** Paint two slanted ovals for eyes. You can change the shape of the eyes to give your skull a different expression, but I like this dopey look on my skull.

**7**

**STEP 7** Paint small black vertical lines at the base of the skull to make the teeth.

## Quick Tip

Don't let your work die like your skull—bury it with a generous layer of topcoat and enjoy!

# Lindsey Williamson
## WONDROUSLY POLISHED

WWW.WONDROUSLYPOLISHED.COM

I'm Lindsey and I like nail polish with a scary passion! I currently live in Southern California with my fiancé, our spoiled-rotten dog, and more nail polish than I'd like to admit to owning. I work as a civil engineer by day and use nail art as a way to relax and unwind from my stressful work life.

I started my blog, *Wondrously Polished*, when I was feeling a bit lost in life. With tons of practice and hard work, my little corner of the Internet has evolved into a collection of my nail art looks, nail polish swatches, tutorials, and random ramblings about my life and experiences. It has also become something I am immensely proud of and has helped me find my voice as an artist and a young woman. In short, my blog has helped me figure out "me" just a little bit more!

I have always been a very meticulous and analytical person, but I also have a creative and artistic side. Nail art allows me to combine these two halves of myself and helps me explore my own unique style. Random textiles, prints, or nature scenes that catch my eye often get translated into a nail art look. I try to stay open-minded—because you never know when creativity might strike!

While nail art consumes a large chunk of my time, I also adore books and obsess over finding that next great read. (I've even done nail art looks inspired by some of my favorite books!) Experimenting with new recipes, enjoying the sound of the rain, spending time with friends and family, and looking at photos of cute baby animals are also favorite pastimes. Overall, I try to do things that make for a wondrously polished life!

# Night Sky

**Balmy summer nights** and stargazing go hand in hand. Whether you're in a city where you can't see the stars or lucky enough to see the Milky Way each night, this night-inspired look is sure to satisfy a love of the beautiful starry sky.

## What You'll Need:

**Brushes—**
- Small dotting tool
- Thin detailing brush

## Quick Tip

Before sponging the polish onto your nail, dab the makeup sponge once or twice onto a piece of paper to remove excess polish. Having less polish on the sponge will help to create texture and depth.

**STEP 1** Start by painting your nails your favorite blue shade, and let the polish dry completely. If you're impatient, add a quick-dry topcoat after this step to speed up the process.

**STEP 2** Begin painting the background of the night sky. Using a makeup sponge, carefully dab a dark indigo polish in the upper portion of each nail. Dab randomly and be sure to let your base polish show through in some areas.

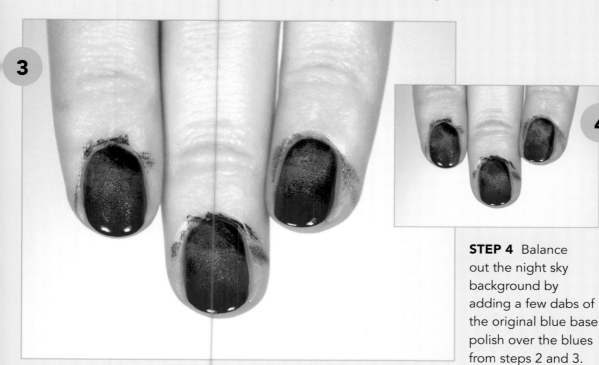

**STEP 4** Balance out the night sky background by adding a few dabs of the original blue base polish over the blues from steps 2 and 3.

**STEP 3** With a light blue or lavender polish, use the same technique as step 2 to randomly sponge this lighter shade over what you've already painted.

**5**

**6**

**STEP 6** On a few nails, add one or two tiny "plus" signs in white. These will look like extra bright stars in the night sky.

**STEP 5** Next are the stars! Use a small dotting tool or toothpick to randomly (and carefully!) paint various-sized dots to create your stars. I use white craft acrylic paint for this step, as you'll avoid smearing your work when you add the topcoat at the end. Add as many stars as you'd like, but keep in mind that sometimes less is more when it comes to this type of design.

**7**

**STEP 7** With black acrylic paint, add the silhouette of a grassy field. Use a thin detailing brush or a toothpick to paint short black lines along the tips of each nail. Alter the length and angle of each line to mimic the look of real grass.

**8**

**STEP 8** Finally, use some polish remover and a cotton swab to carefully clean up any polish that may have gotten on your skin during the painting process. Finish up by adding your favorite topcoat, and enjoy your work!

### Quick Tip

The possibilities for landscape nail designs are endless. Once you master the night sky, give this more challenging watercolor vista a try.

# Simple Flowers

No matter the time of year, a simple and cute flower manicure is never a bad thing. The best part? You can change up the color palette to create a floral look that works year-round!

## What You'll Need:

### Brushes—
- Small dotting tool
- Thin detailing brush

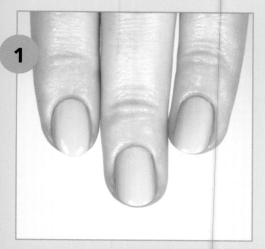

**STEP 1** Paint your nails with a light lavender polish, and let dry completely.

**STEP 2** Next grab your white polish and a small dotting tool. On each nail, add a ring of six dots, evenly spaced from each other. These are the start of your flower petals.

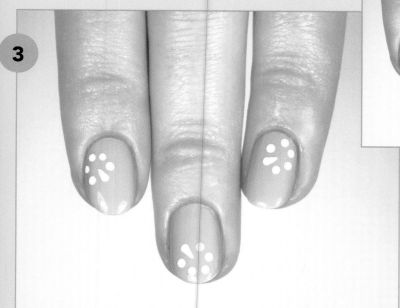

**STEP 4** Repeat this step on each of the other dots until you have a full flower. If your petals touch each other in a few places, don't worry! You'll still have a cute mani at the end.

**STEP 3** With a detailing brush or a toothpick, paint a small triangle shape on the inside of one of the dots. This creates a teardrop shape (like a petal).

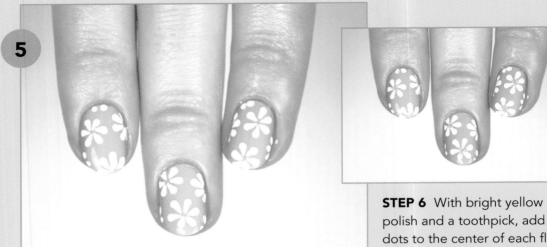

**STEP 6** With bright yellow polish and a toothpick, add three dots to the center of each flower. Finally, use your favorite topcoat to protect your hard work!

**STEP 5** Repeat steps 3 and 4 to create several flowers on each nail. Get creative with your placement, and have some of the flowers peeking off the edge of your nail.

## Purple Petals

Consider yourself a modern flower child? Pair your springtime nails with these floral beauties.

# Basic Paisley

*Paisley will always be in style* when you're wearing it on your nails. While this version of paisley is fairly basic, the sky is the limit when it comes to the different variations you can put together. Use these basic shapes and techniques as a starting point to get creative and paint something unique to you.

## What You'll Need:

### Brushes—
- Detailing brush
- Small dotting tool
- Large dotting tool

**STEP 1** Start with a nude-colored base polish, and let dry completely.

**STEP 2** Grab your detail brush and a light blue polish, and carefully paint a twisted teardrop shape on each nail. This is the quintessential paisley pattern shape so take your time to get it looking just right.

**STEP 3** Add blue dots to the entire outside edge of the shapes. You can use a small dotting tool or even a toothpick.

**4**

**STEP 4** With black polish and your detailing brush, add a smaller teardrop shape inside the first one.

**5**

**STEP 5** Use a larger dotting tool to add a big dot in the bottom of the black teardrop.

**6**

**STEP 6** If you have the room, add a few more basic paisley shapes on the rest of your nails. Keep these simple with solid lines and minimal dots.

**7**

**STEP 7** Finally, fill in the surrounding blank space with some white dots to finish up the look. Add a topcoat and enjoy!

# Abstract Roses

**Whether you're into** an edgy look or something a bit more dainty and feminine, these abstract roses work for everyone! Keep your roses traditional with pink and red petals, or go crazy with blue or purple roses over a fun, contrasting background color.

## What You'll Need:

**Brushes—**
- Small dotting tool
- Detailing brush

**STEP 1** Start by painting your nails with your favorite black polish, and let them dry completely to avoid smudges.

**STEP 2** With a small dotting tool and some coral or pink polish, add a small dot on each nail. This will be the center of your rose.

**STEP 4** Add three more petals outside the ones you just painted. Try to offset the petals so that each outside petal begins and ends at the midpoint of an inside petal.

**STEP 3** Carefully use the dotting tool to paint three small, kidney bean shapes around the center dot. Try to leave gaps between the petals.

**5**

**6**

**STEP 6** Finally, with a bright green polish, dab on a few leaves for each flower. This will pull the whole look together. Finish up with a topcoat and enjoy your hard work!

**STEP 5** Depending on the look you're going for (or how much nail space you have left!), add a few more roses to each nail.

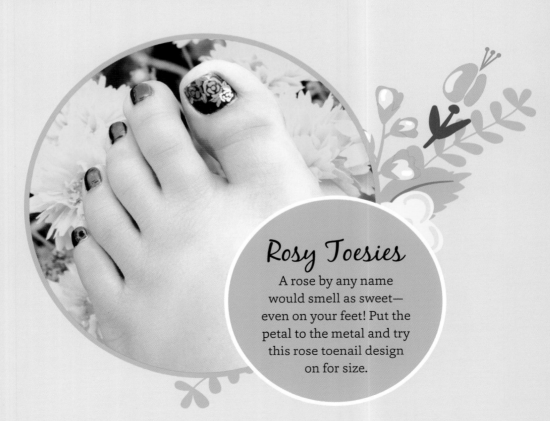

## Rosy Toesies

A rose by any name would smell as sweet— even on your feet! Put the petal to the metal and try this rose toenail design on for size.

## Quick Tip

Use various shades of pink for each petal to add even more interest to your look! If your petals accidentally touch, don't sweat it! Just take a detailing brush and your base polish, and carefully paint back over any errors you made.

# Mosaic

**Geometric designs are always** eye-catching and fun to wear—and this mosaic technique is bound to wow anyone who sees it! A full manicure with this design is shown here, but if doing all your nails feels daunting, it's a great technique to use for an accent nail instead. Try mixing up the color palette to fit your mood (or the time of year).

## What You'll Need:

### Brushes—
- Small dotting tool
- Detailing brush

**STEP 1** Before you begin, apply a coat or two of your favorite base coat. Once that is dry, use a long striping brush and some white polish to randomly paint geometric outlines on each nail. Don't worry about how straight or clean your lines are—you can fix them in the last step!

**STEP 2** Grab your first polish, and carefully fill in some of the shapes you created in step 1. Don't fill too many in just yet, as you want to make sure you have room to add all the other colors in the following steps.

**STEP 3** Choose a second polish shade, and fill in a few more shapes.

**STEP 4** Again, use a third polish to paint a few more areas.

**STEP 5** With the last polish, fill in the remaining shapes. If you have some spaces left unpainted, go back and fill them in with some of the previous polishes. Make sure there is no bare nail showing.

**STEP 6** Finally, with your white polish and striping brush, go back over the lines between the shapes. This creates the crisp detail that you find in mosaic art. Finish up the look with your favorite topcoat, and clean up any excess polish around your cuticles with a cotton swab dipped in acetone.

# Stained Glass

Once you've mastered the mosaic concept from the previous design, consider giving this more complex look a try! This stained glass design uses the same simple lines used in the mosaic look (this time with black polish), but instead of a random pattern, we'll create a picture. With practice, you'll find that you can transform almost anything into stained glass!

## What You'll Need:

Brushes—
- Detailing brush

**1**

**STEP 1** After applying your base coat, use a black polish (or black acrylic paint) to paint the outline of a flower. Start with the outlines of the stem, and then add in the petals. Don't worry if it's not perfect—you can adjust things later.

**2**

**STEP 2** Add some dimension to the backdrop by painting horizontal and angled lines directly behind the flower.

**3**

**4**

**STEP 4** Next use bright blue polish to create the sky backdrop. With green polish, paint the stem.

**STEP 3** With red polish, carefully fill in each flower petal. If you'd like, use various shades of red on different petals.

**STEP 5** On your remaining nails, paint some grass to create one, cohesive image. At the tip of each nail, paint the outlines of grass shooting up your nail.

**STEP 6** Define the skyline a bit more by adding vertical lines above the grass. The lines might look a bit random right now, but the next step will make things clearer!

**STEP 7** With the green polish, fill in the blades of grass at the tip of each nail. Use the same blue polish from step 4 to fill in the sky.

**STEP 8** Finally, go back over your initial outlines with your black polish and detailing brush. If you'd like, add additional lines to break up the sky a bit more. Finish up the look by outlining each nail with a solid black line. This will frame your nail like a real piece of stained-glass artwork!

## Quick Tip

Use a cleanup brush and pure acetone to clean up around your nails, and add a layer of quick-dry topcoat for seal and shine.

# Cutout Gradient

A gradient is one of the most eye-catching and fun ways to gussy up your nails. Incorporating some negative space into that gradient is a great update to a classic nail art technique and will make everyone take a second glance. Are you more of a pink girl? Or maybe you like shades of black and gray? Either way, this mani can work for you! You can use any colors you'd like!

## What You'll Need:

**Brushes—**
- Striping tape

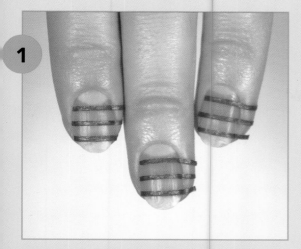

**STEP 1** Start with freshly cleaned nails and apply your favorite base coat. Using three pieces of striping tape, section off your nails into four different areas. If you don't have striping tape, carefully cut pieces of masking tape into strips like I've done instead!

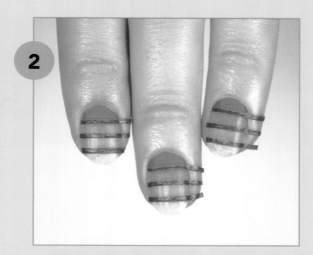

**STEP 2** Next up, choose your color scheme. I've gone with a dark teal to white look, but pick your colors depending on your mood. With your darkest polish, carefully paint the bottom portion of your taped-off nail.

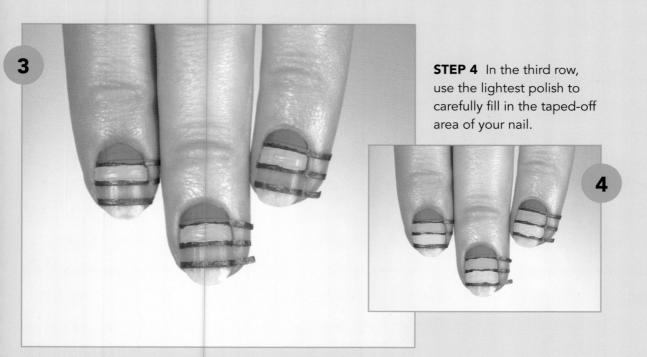

**STEP 4** In the third row, use the lightest polish to carefully fill in the taped-off area of your nail.

**STEP 3** Paint the second row with your next darkest shade.

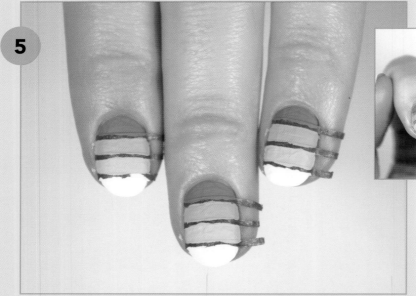

**5**

**STEP 5** Finally, with white polish, paint the tips of each nail.

**6**

**STEP 6** Carefully remove the strips of tape to reveal your look. If any of the polish bled under the tape, don't worry! Take an angled brush and some acetone, and carefully remove the polish that found its way into the negative space.

## Green with Envy

You'll be the envy of all your friends with this lean, green cutout gradient toenail design. Use diagonal stripes for a slightly easier art deco design.

## Quick Tip

If you don't have enough colors to make this mani work—don't fret! All you really need is white polish and a dark polish in the color you want. On a piece of scrap paper, dab out some of the dark polish, and add a small drop of white to it. Mix these together to create your second darkest shade. Repeat this step for the second lightest color by adding two to three drops of white to the original dark polish. This allows you to create the varying shades you need for the look.

# INSPIRATION GALLERY

Celine Does Nails

Jessica Washick of
U Need a Manicure

Adventures In Acetone

Celine Does Nails

Adventures In Acetone

Adventures In Acetone

Celine Does Nails

Celine Does Nails

Jessica Washick of
U Need a Manicure

# DESIGN TEMPLATES

Photocopy these templates to create your own original nail art designs.

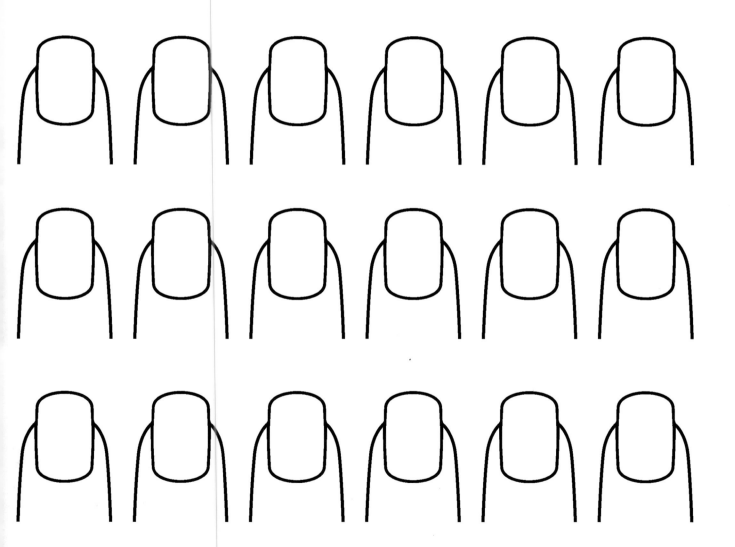

# Penelope Yee

WWW.INSTAGRAM.COM/JOVIALWEAVER

 All my life, I was a nail biter. I distinctly remember watching a suspenseful movie, and then looking down at my short, bleeding nails to realize I'd been biting them the entire time.

Things changed in high school. Working as a receptionist, I felt ashamed of my unkempt nails. I decided, "That's it—no more biting!" Knowing that ragged, sharp nails were my worst enemy, I started painting my nails religiously. Practice makes perfect, and my polish collection grew steadily.

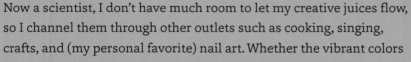

Now a scientist, I don't have much room to let my creative juices flow, so I channel them through other outlets such as cooking, singing, crafts, and (my personal favorite) nail art. Whether the vibrant colors and organic lines of Mother Nature, the clean geometry found in architecture, or a bright, striking print on a dress, I find beauty in everything and try to incorporate it into my art. I keep up with nail trends and try the latest techniques to keep things fresh. Inspiration is everywhere! An open mind and the willingness to try something new are all you need. And hey, if you don't like what you've done on your nails, one swipe of remover and voilà! Your canvases are ready for a new creation.